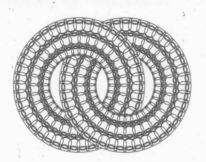

In

the

River

of

Songs

In the River of Songs

SUSAN JACKSON

CAVANKERRY
PRESS

CavanKerry Press Ltd.
Fort Lee, New Jersey
www.cavankerrypress.org

Publisher's Cataloging-In-Publication Data
(Prepared by The Donohue Group, Inc.)
Names: Jackson, Susan, 1947- author.
Title: In the river of songs / Susan Jackson.
Description: First edition. | Fort Lee, New Jersey : CavanKerry Press, 2022.
Identifiers: ISBN 9781933880921
Subjects: LCSH: Families—Poetry. | Spirituality—Poetry. | Loss
    (Psychology)—Poetry. | Nature—Psychological aspects—Poetry. |
    LCGFT: Poetry.
Classification: LCC PS3610.A35525 I5 2022 | DDC 811/.6—dc23

Cover artwork: Early on the River, 2010. Copyright John Evans.
    Courtesy the artist and Gallery Henoch, New York
Cover and interior text design by Ryan Scheife, Mayfly Design
First Edition 2022, Printed in the United States of America

CAVANKERRY
PRESS

 Made possible by funds from the
New Jersey State Council on the Arts, a partner
agency of the National Endowment for the Arts.

CavanKerry Press is grateful for the support it receives
from the New Jersey State Council on the Arts.

In addition, CavanKerry Press gratefully acknowledges generous
emergency support received during the COVID-19 pandemic
from the following funders:

Community of Literary Magazines and Presses

New Jersey Arts and Culture Recovery Fund

New Jersey Council for the Humanities

New Jersey Economic Development Authority

Northern New Jersey Community Foundation

The Poetry Foundation

US Small Business Administration

Also by Susan Jackson

Through a Gate of Trees (2007)
All the Light in Between (2013)

for my family

Contents

I. Echo of the Former World

The Woman Who Loved Trees 3

All the Light in Between 5

What I Heard My Mother Say Before I Was Born 6

Pausing Below Inspiration Point, Jenny Lake 7

A Hundred Ravens 9

Honey 11

El Anatsui 12

From Under the Eaves 13

Clementine 15

Making Beds 16

The Funnel 18

The Story of Light 20

Perseid Meteor Showers 21

Pockets Full of Stones 22

A Poem Is the Sky 24

II. Early on the River

So Big Was Her Kindness 27

Rain, Higuera Blanca 28

Letter Home 30

Soufflé 32

Through the Glass Bottom Boat of the Mind 33

On the Death of a Childhood Friend 34

What Goes Among the Things That Change 36

Quicksilver 38

Mother in the Alzheimer's Wing 40

Benediction of the Four Birds, New Year's Day 42

Let It Be Felt the Painter Was There 44

My Body 45

III. Haying Time

Anything with Wings 49

The Nourishment of Childhood 51

Praise 52

John Henry 53

Ode to a Boiled Egg 55

Song II, Punta del Burro 56

Instructions for Comfort Care 57

Massage 58

Offering of the Bear Paw Bowl 59

Elk 60

Doing the Jigsaw Puzzle 61

What If Every Poem Were a Prayer 62

Notes 65

Acknowledgments 67

I

Echo of the Former World

The Woman Who Loved Trees

The woman who loved trees
couldn't bear to see the cottonwoods taken down

though their roots had gone wild
pushing stones onto the terrace

strangling underground wires;
she walked the garden talking to the trees

weighted to think of losing
the patterns of light along the pathway

but the body needs to bend, to yield,
liquefy as light liquefies hills

and here's the mystery:
she *was* a woman who loved trees,

but next day the cottonwoods were gone,
the yard empty;

this emptiness flowed
over the walkway

to fill the space,
became a singing bowl;

maybe the ground already felt
the coming of something new,

maybe solitude became her companion
in her changed landscape

for the woman who loved trees
also loved rosemary and cosmos,

wild lupine, and the quaking aspen
turning golden in the distance

All the Light in Between

I stand transfixed at the window
listening to the sound of water,
watching a hawk circle—
this is the moment when color deepens
around the mountains
the way your eyes do sometimes
when you feel moved.
It's late. Some sunlight still shimmers,
reluctant to go down
as I too am reluctant to leave this moment
after we have loved.
Reluctant to pick up the salad bowl,
tear the lettuce, light the stove and the lamps,
let my attention move from diffused
to focused, the sun on me
and all the light in between.

What I Heard My Mother Say Before I Was Born

A black snake has shed its skin on the back steps.
The shedding I heard in my mother's body

like untangling a fish from a line—that must be
where I first learned how to be in the world.

I was the whoosh of water and had no voice yet;
she sang to me and I could feel her

breathe, feel her sit our heaviness down
on the red sofa, lift her legs to the long footstool

as she disconnected from life around us;
I could hear time threading

through the string of days, collecting me into her
world, her words like incantations,

those sounds of loosening
in the home we shared.

Light passing through water creates a prism—
I reach out to catch the colors as they disappear

between my fingers. *Wild*, I think I hear her say,
joy. What I'll be born to—like frogs jumping,

lively, exuberant, free. Then she whispers, *oh
please God, let my baby be okay*

but then I wasn't

Pausing Below Inspiration Point, Jenny Lake

Honestly I'm scared to death

     on this narrow ledge

          when I see how far down the lake is

none of the other hikers

     seem aware of the drop

          not the woman in flip-flops

nor the man with a toddler

     on his shoulders

          even when his foot slips

and sends a stone hurling

     through space

          that sound alone makes me

huddle closer to the rock wall

     my friends have gone on

          up, also oblivious

a voice in my head

      claiming to be the mountain (!)

            says *don't look down*

look out

      at the beauty

            you will not fall

and this is just too weird

      my other self thinks

            but I remember what Bashō said

when he crossed the great divide

      to tell the truth is a miracle

            which is when I unfreeze

enough to stand up, rise

      like Jacob from his pillow

            this is holy ground

and maybe that's all I need to know

      to follow these steep paths

            along earth's ancient body

A Hundred Ravens

At the art fair
she loves a painting of spring flowers
by Richard Schmid

and another artist's work called
A Hundred Ravens.
I notice she's perspiring,

then watch her body sink,
as if in slow motion, like a tunnel
collapsing onto the floor.

Sirens. Paramedics try
but nothing they can do
will save her life.

Her stricken husband
holding on to her hand.
The rest of us huddle

together, stunned into silence.
Even today the potency
of that afternoon lives in me

and can bring me to tears,
which is what is happening,
when suddenly I hear

the sound of wings,
and as if out of that painting
I see a hundred ravens

fly across the valley
between the Tetons
and the Sleeping Indian

to the top of our hill
and all along the ridgeline
where copper-colored lichens

cover the rocks
above the sagebrush
and the split rail fence.

The sound of wings, the long call
of the ravens. Then quiet
except for the wind.

Honey

As soon as we spread honey on our toast,
two bees buzz the table
and won't leave
for anything. They zoom. They perch on plates.
The man says he's allergic and wants to wave
them away but the woman says that only aggravates them
and the children start to scream for fear of being stung.
It's a madhouse.
All the delight of our family breakfast on a terrace
overlooking the Bay of Banderas with hummingbirds
delving into red hibiscus and the sound of the sea
gone because of honey.
Then the woman spoons a dollop on a saucer
at the far end of the table and we let the creatures join us.
For the rest of breakfast the bees feast
like beings returned to their own creation.
The honey is golden. We watch it glisten in the sun
while bee legs jig with delight and they feed
as if that's all there is.

El Anatsui

As I open the wine tonight and tear away
the bottle's metal collar
I think of Anatsui collecting all the caps and tabs,
pieces of old soda cans from African ground
and making art—those long curtains of metal
stitched together, gleaming with *Gravity and Grace.*

Today I cut the last three peonies
before the rain came
and by evening they've drooped, petals dropping
onto the kitchen counter one by one.

So what lasts?
All the people of my family are gone
and mourned and I am alone save for you.

But there's a place that Anatsui knew:
that empty space like the invisible hub
at the center of an ever-turning wheel
where out of nothing creation flows
birthing art into our world.

From Under the Eaves

we watch the fledgling wrens
leave the nest,
each waiting on the stone wall
beside the house
before flying off

then a weasel appears
from a crevice in the rocks,
the mother wren
dive-bombs his head
and he hides for a minute
but pops out closer
while parent birds peck him back

it's the 50th anniversary
of the moon landing
and someone sent me
the words the president
would have read
if the men were not able
to return to earth—
the piece praised
the astronauts' valor,
told how they went in peace,
laying down their lives
in search of truth and understanding

and I think
about the day the Challenger
blew up in '86,
how we watched it live
on TV at Sloan Kettering

in the time of your brain tumor;
as they wheeled you
into the elevator for surgery
you raised your hand to wave
and then the door closed

Clementine

The paring knife circles the top,
frees a round, orange roof with a
nodule in the center where the stem was,
like a beret I can lift off whole;

as I peel the rind,
oil of citrus coats my fingertips,
the fragrance not hovering in my nose only
but jigging through my body
like some kind of dance.

As I pull away sections
and hand them to you one by one
you smile; all that can be said
is said in silence. This
is what I want to remember—
what I will remember always—
the moment, and our shared fruit.

Making Beds

My husband's mother, dead these thirty years,
yet she stands across from me
as I bend to tuck the blanket.

Here we are again, our younger selves
on opposite sides of her bed.
As we pull the top sheet over the semen stain,

we are silent and don't meet each other's eyes,
tacit in our knowing the ways of couples.
I am so young I believe I know.

I never made my mother's bed but went there on a sick day
home from school, in the night with dreams, to open stockings
on Christmas morning and find the orange deep in the toe.

Mother used her mother's sheets,
Egyptian cotton hemstitched by hand
before the days of wrinkle-free, and gathered

the children to her bed to read them stories
at nighttime. She brought a tray with white
linen when I came home from hospital

after the new baby died. I never wanted to get out
of that bed—how could I bear to tell the children
there was no little brother coming home.

I touched my mother's sheets again
when she lay dying, my hand
on her hand across the bed.

I smoothed and tucked those sheets and pillows,
whispering how she was loved, but her bed
was a white boat and she already sailing away.

The Funnel

From the wideness of your

   living world

death funnels you

   into one room

     and a bed.

Dust motes

   form a line of light

    from the bedside table

lamp;

outside snow begins to fall

   but that means nothing

now.

Like a birthing mother

   the body

has a path to follow

   surrendering the intricate operations

one by one

like the careful housekeeper

going from room to room

   turning out lights

drawing curtains.

You briefly

   raise one hand

as if

   in greeting.

The Story of Light

on the table by the window
in the clay pot of white lilies
light shines through each individual petal
erasing the edges of the separate
leaves and stems, revealing
a living light inside the plant itself
and though I could never have imagined
this happening away from you
it creates in me another kind of knowing
as if I could remember some inner beauty of my own
I would never otherwise have known I had

Perseid Meteor Showers

Night is calling—

the mountain air is cold

through your thin nightie,

to your bare feet,

but go outside anyway.

Now look north

east of Andromeda

south of Cassiopeia

where you see the long trails

as they flare, burn up,

and disappear

and the stars

stretching out

boundless

and you, alone in the night

with a dazzling gift

all because you came outside.

Pockets Full of Stones

for Virginia Woolf (1882–1941)

She visits me in winter.
We walk the long stretch of beach together
companions gathering stones.

Listen, she says,
the stones have voices—
it's not just the sound of waves

washing over them
tide and foam
pulling, tumbling them back

the stones remember the tossing
that broke them open
then made them smooth

she tells me
as she bends down to pick one up
I do also, pausing

to hold the perfect,
round, cold stone
and put it in my pocket

and she does too
bending a kind of kneeling,
as they slip into her coat pockets

we talk about the voices
about the unseen force
patron saint of tears

my stones will stay on my desk
like a tune I carry
they carry the song of the sea

but she loads them into
her pockets and walks
straight into the water

I want to shout at her
don't do it
she's knee-deep now

I reach out to grab her arm
but she's gone, a phantom
who disappears and

how she came is a mystery
but the why—
she came to remind me

about the lighthouse.

A Poem Is the Sky

First light behind bare tree branches

and the way invisible writing appears on paper
I see the tracks

left by the red fox
in the frost on the grass

a jay flies from the blue spruce
toward the curve of white moon

and the sky is a poem.

II

Early on the River

So Big Was Her Kindness

I know Mother must have tucked me in at night
but who I remember most is Maggie.
People say it's not right to take a woman away
from her own children to nurse someone else's
but that's the way it was for us.
I loved her.

Mother said *sit still!* when I fidgeted
as she brushed my hair. Maggie wove my
braids so the gold strands showed
and called them a gift from the angels.
After school she let us take

our shoes and socks off
to wade in the stream bed,
the fluid cool around my legs.
She taught us to skip stones—
magic how she made them
hop across the water.

She tendered me.
If I couldn't sleep, she rocked me
until I felt like the earth after rain.
For fevers a wet washcloth sprinkled with lemon
and lavender. So big was her kindness
I could let her love my sister too.

Rain, Higuera Blanca

the way night erases

day

this small hotel

cantilevered out

over the ocean

like a bird

perched on the outermost

branch of a *huanacaxtle* tree

surf pounds rocks

harmonica and guitar

tuned to the

skitterish sound of rain

splashing off rooftops

like jujubes jumping

on the leaves

on the blue stone pavement

rivulets pattern

window glass

lightning flash

brights

the whole room

your face

our taste

of the infinite

so why not

use the word

bliss

Letter Home

Thank you for asking
if I could hear the sound of the river
from my room. I know I said no,
but last night
I opened the window
and through the open window
the river lapping lulled me to sleep.
All night the voice of water flowing
flowed through the riverbed and me.
All night dreams dreamed me
a story
our accordion ways
together and apart
the shape of us
ripples in the river
in my hand
a stone with ancient letters
from another language
a poem I try
to decipher
like the mystery of us
we stand
in the center
of a prehistoric
stone circle
there's the glimmer
of a code
a kind of Braille
I feel but

don't know
how to say
your voice
my wonder
bright, bright

Soufflé

In the yard on a summer day
a child dips the wand into the cup,

raises it to the sky,
and gently blows—

too hard the liquid disperses,
too soft it dribbles to the ground.

Soufflé the French would say
for the tender motion of wind

and the child knows
how it feels like whistling

and watches the bubble expands
then floats off
a perfect iridescence   rising   soaring

shimmering   then—*pop!*—gone
the child does it again and again

dipping the wand, creating those fragile spheres
every time full of surprise when one bursts

here and gone   disappearing just like that
just like us—

rise shimmer gone
rise shimmer gone

Through the Glass Bottom Boat of the Mind

Like rows of miniature Xi'an warriors

or little corn husk stalks—

the tulips were left late this year

to dry in the sun,

send power back to the bulb.

As I cut them down

they crinkle, rustle

like a taffeta petticoat.

Lying in the basket

they look like mummies

in the Museum of Antiquities

in Cairo or an old parchment map

charting the unknown.

Seems no time since we watched

hot pink and peach-colored blossoms,

tapered apple-green leaves

bobble on their stems

and nod in the afternoon breeze.

On the Death of a Childhood Friend

He says his stomach hurts
but she thinks he's sad at the news,
remembering this friend
as a little boy, how he accidentally shot
a bird with the air gun birthday present
and how the two boys cried.
They cried for the power of death
and its deceptiveness
because the bird
looked so still and whole
and then they felt ashamed of their tears.

His father was dead too
and his mother buried
in another country.
Over the years
the loneliness of the boy
becomes the loneliness
of the man.
That's what he can't stomach.
And there it is when his friend dies
and he can't cry.

What can a woman do
for a man like this?
He is calling—
but for what?

For something he doesn't even know—
maybe for a blessing to be cast
over all these losses,

maybe a wish for the world
to feel porous and pure,
maybe just for him to be able to believe
it *could* be that way.

What Goes Among the Things That Change

with a line by William Stafford

I always thought it was the breath,
the faithful breath
coming in and going out,
and when I followed it with my heart
it calmed me.

Then the sound of sirens
on narrow streets
and wide avenues of the great cities
so many people with the sickness
not able to breathe.
Then one man:

I can't breathe
he cried

calling for his mother

but the knee is still on him

I   can't   breathe

                              please

calling
until he couldn't
anymore.

Now
it's the world that must breathe for him.
It's the breath
that walks the streets at night

in the silent dark, or shouts
by the light
of bonfires
and burning cars.

The breath of prayers
and voices
say
enough, dignity, justice,
the talk of peace
in this time of people
breathing together.

Quicksilver

Mother dropped us off
so she could run errands.
In the dentist's office
of my childhood
the dentist himself was called
Dr. Payne. Even a nine-year-old knew
he should change his name.
He told bad jokes
as he prodded and probed
with the gleaming machinery.

But if I'd been a good girl,
and I always was,
he bestowed another gift—
a pea-sized mercurial ball
called quicksilver
which roamed the palm
of my hand like a piece of gunshot.
I watched it divide
into tiny bits when provoked
with my fingernail, then reassemble
as one quivering silver orb when I
rotated my hand back and forth.
All through my sister's turn in the grim chair
with the screaming drill
I waited in the waiting room
where I could hear something
deep in her throat—
not a moan really—
more like gagging.
Again and again my index finger
jabbed the little ball of quicksilver

to break it apart
and I watched how it whizzed back together
as if drawn by some invisible
magnetic shining inside itself.

If meaning had a rhythm
or a tune it could sing,
what would it be I hummed
to the shimmering quicksilver?
Tell me your secret, I marveled,
oblivious to its dangerous nature
capable of poisoning
anyone who touched it.

Mother in the Alzheimer's Wing

Already it's like sitting with her ghost, this woman who
    spends her days
in the mists of other worlds, not even knowing where she
    lives.

Her eyes the color of cattails, reflective like still water,
but she looks beyond me toward that other, far side of the air,

brushes back wisps of silver hair and sighs. But when I sing my
    favorite childhood songs
she chimes in softly and doesn't look surprised (as I am)

to know the words. Once she bustled in hospital nurseries
    tending to newborns.
I wish she remembered those days; I want her to tell me her
    stories again

so I don't forget, *so I keep you with me, Mother* . . . but now her
    eyes close,
she coughs, like the seven black crows on the grass outside
    caw caw,

and she flies out of sight where I can't reach her. Sometimes I
    feel her in me
as I bend over the kitchen counter to read, crossing my ankles

and leaning on my elbows the way she always did—as if my
    body knows
what connects us—just now she opens her eyes and says
    clearly

You're my daughter, right? and when I say yes, she answers
Good!

then goes right back to sleep. And here I thought this poem
   was about what's lost

but instead turns out to be for every unexpected gift we're
   given.

Benediction of the Four Birds,
New Year's Day

for my daughter Alexandra

It's the day before your visit ends—
    your last swim before packing
        and we float dreamy, weightless,

easy as skiffs on the water's surface
    everything glittering
        in late afternoon sun

when the kiskadees come to land
    on the pool's edge. Right beside us
        birds bend their heads

to drink from the cool water
    like apparitions
        of primrose-yellow.

They skim and dip, unafraid;
    we don't dare move,
        for how long I can't say,

like time out of time,
    a wedge of eternity,
        and we wonder why they've come—

perhaps to simply bless us
    with their presence,
        or maybe a message . . .

but here we are in Nayarit
  beginning the New Year
    believing in goodness

and we are not alone

Let It Be Felt the Painter Was There

for Pierre Bonnard

Let it be felt the painter was there,
wrote Bonnard, artist of the floating world
he captured on canvas in a gospel of shapes.
Whether studying the cadence of space
through *The French Window*
or in *The Terrace at Vernon*
he made an altarpiece
of the sudden moment of seeing . . .
and still, he wanted us to know the unseen hand,
the man himself in search of the pure thing;
as colors pitched and winked
he found rapport between the green and blue,
the peach and cornhusk yellow,
brushstrokes creating the new language for what he saw and felt
in the mystery of light and shadow. His wife Marthe
with *The Bowl of Milk*, Marthe at the table, or legs spread
on the unmade bed, Marthe
in the water of so many tubs, cradled—
he didn't search out beauty—the how and why of beauty
was what he saw and what he loved, the seduction of his art.

My Body

As I fell asleep last night
I felt the blood pulse through my body
and from nowhere came
thank you

I thought of service,
the way these legs carry me
from place to place, the symmetry of twos
and the dependable breath all these years.

Oh my heart, are you the seat
of all this love—

and what about the leather-bound book
some revere as holy;
it may be older than my body

but it cannot even dance or sing,
be dazzled by the gathering sky,
or cradle any living thing in its arms.

I muse over how this body of mine
metabolizes what comes,
withstands the change of season
and circumstance,

births every sort of creation—
what a companion
for my solitary soul,
which swells now beyond itself
and bows with appreciation.

III

Haying Time

Anything with Wings

Anything with wings
reminded me of Mother
after she died—
even a honey bee at the window
hovering and buzzing
or the hummingbird dipping
to the deep blooms
on the terrace,
butterflies, birds—bluebirds
all indigo iridescence,
and the call of the cardinal
bell-like over the world—
how she loved their sudden winter red
on snow

some say a person passing
away is like the wing
of a library burning down—
all those stories, the history,
so many pages perished—

but after the burning
this afternoon
on our walk
a wind comes up
trees take wing
their leaves shimmer
in sunlight winking
in this wind
dogwood petals fly

like wings beating air
these threads of light
all the white wings
like you
everywhere

The Nourishment of Childhood

I remember those casseroles that came when Daddy died—
Aunt Marion's chicken tetrazzini,
Mrs. Nickerson's spaghetti
with meatballs and marinara sauce.
Joyce Nelson's butterscotch brownies
and strawberry shortcake.
We ate their kindness
every evening in the dark hours
as Mother read aloud
the cards that came
from people
remembering him.
I never heard him
sing in the church choir
in Orange
or saw him hit a home run
on the baseball diamond
in Derby.
I never knew
he paid
for funerals
and hospital bills
of people I never met.
But here were all these letters
telling us of his quiet
benevolence,
and their stories
became ladders
I could use to climb up
out of grief,
like unexpected guests
come to ransom me.

Praise

Praise for the drops of rain after days of drought.
Praise from the thirsty plants, the green leaves
of the silver birch, the parched dry earth now singing
in mud. Even the earthworms deep in the soil churn
with delight. Crepe myrtle blossoms
like small cups collecting beads of water.
Everything from the dahlias to the cosmos,
to the Heavenly Blue morning glories
climbing the back fence, everything that grows
seems to be saying thank you.

We are not looking down to measure amounts.
We are raising our faces to the rain. We are letting
the children stomp in puddles even when they splash
everything from the tips of their red rain boots to the knees
of their worn jeans, and the grown-ups—we are cupping
our outstretched hands to feel the soft wet
and for once simply feeling happy.

John Henry

Only years later could we come to name you.
Only after some silent passage of time
could we hold the loss
in our fragile woven basket
strand by strand
no match we thought for the weight
of pain deep in our bellies.

Losing you came before we freed each other
from what had been graven into our cells:
what isn't talked about will go away,
won't be real, but it was real, only hidden
and what is hidden has power
over even the land of everyday
with its invisible chore work
folding sheets and towels into neat stacks,
drying dishes, one mug nested in another,
all the tasks only noticed when left undone.
One day as I shook the bread crumbs
off the tablecloth, from the back porch
onto the grass for birds to feed, that day
I saw flickers of light.

Once while cutting branches from the red hibiscus,
already a bouquet of blooms in my left hand,
a hummingbird came to them. So close
the whir of wings fanned the sweetened air
over my face and arm. I held my breath.

To give you a name now
is like an exhale. Like the completion
of a cycle of sorrow. We breathe out so that
we can breathe in, begin again, and again.
Like an offering. Our song of lament
rises.

Ode to a Boiled Egg

Perfect in its ovid entirety, hot, brown,
tucked into a flowered porcelain eggcup
my husband brings me on a tray in bed.
Beside the egg a spoon, some sea salt, a piece
of sourdough toast with the crusts cut off.
My husband took the time to do this.

I picture him downstairs in the white kitchen
opening drawers, looking for the perfect knife,
turning the toast on the wooden cutting board
as he slices off each crunchy crust.
The toast glistens with butter.
He has thought of everything.
I tap the top of the hot brown egg
with the back of my spoon—*splat—crack—*
and lift off a slice
like a little hat from the egg.
The white shimmies, then sits still to hold
the pool of deep golden yellow.

A boiled egg. This offering my husband has made for me
all by himself. Tender and soft in the center.
Little curls of steam rise as I dip my spoon deeper in.
It is delicious. It is just right. One boiled egg
and this tenderness will make me well.

Song II, Punta del Burro

I'll never climb the stairs again without seeing
the snake on the landing—ribbon thin,

color of a reed. It lay there, head raised like a cobra,
the position ancient Egyptians called divine

but when you meet a snake in your house
it doesn't feel divine. You scream for help.

You don't take your eyes off the creature
lest it dart out of sight under furniture or in a closet

and you have to go to sleep at night knowing
somewhere there's a snake.

The man came running. Brought a rake
and a bag, then the snake tried to escape behind

the big planter. It got caught,
but when afternoon sunlight casts shadows

over the stone floor or wind disturbs the palm fronds,
I shiver.

Instructions for Comfort Care

Let the natural passage out of the world
be as painless as possible
allow a slipping away
without doing artificial things
the soul may feel as
tugging at her coattails
let her go
let her pass gently
into the other world
let her be loved as she goes
let someone hold her hand
let soothing sound
like prayer or song accompany her
let her lips be moistened
let her know it's all right
when the time has come
let her know there's no need
to say good-bye

Massage

Oil soothes my shoulders,
neck, and finally the back loosens,

lets its history go as hands convince
the faithful tissues *release, relax.*

A taste as thick as longing rises,
then belly, arms, and legs go languid.

Time slips from the twilight room
and what's left? Only the ordinary

eloquence with which the body speaks its story—
finally enough just being as I am

naked on the table, the white towel,
me in my own skin.

Offering of the Bear Paw Bowl

for Maria Margarita "Margaret" Tafoya,
Santa Clara Pueblo

Take this bowl
in both your hands.
Close your eyes
and let your fingers
follow the circumference.
Feel the cool, smooth surface
soft as silk over skin,
then trace the bear paw carved
at each of the four directions.

Imagine gathering the clay,
listening for a shape
only the clay knows.
Feel it squish in your palms;
as you work the coils form,

the vessel turns.
Strong hands for the smoothing
and fire making, time for the tending,

listening for the blue voice
to tell when the piece is cooked.
Do you sing as the stone
burnishes the bowl?
Can you see your face
in the new luster?

Elk

They came into the field without a sound,
stood there watching us

with grace and the kind of gaze humans hold
when it's love at first sight.

Antlers like outstretched arms
reaching to the heavens.

I wanted to go to them. Something wild
you know you can't touch,

but still some border had been crossed
between them and us. They stayed

so completely unafraid, their presence
like a gift asking nothing in return.

Another and another emerged
from the stand of aspens

until I felt the urge to count them all
as if numbers could contain

what words failed—
this unseen force

as day was ending,
in the blue hour

as dusk fell over our valley
in Wyoming.

Doing the Jigsaw Puzzle

van Gogh's Sea at Saintes-Maries

My house has been torn down—
no going back now.
In dreams I visit the dry bones

where wind echoes
over the empty space

and nothing's left
but the mother rock,
pattern of tides, skies of fire,
these threads that hold me
to the earth.

In the mackerel light van Gogh loved
I sort through each found truth
looking for its right order
and place

in this puzzle of who I am—

house of joy
house of sorrow

a mosaic—

and each faithful piece,
particular to the touch,
comes together
to form a radiant whole.

What If Every Poem Were a Prayer

The face of the river is also changing
   after last night's storm.
      Skeletons of trees float downstream,

their trunks like bones bleached white
   by weather as they let themselves be carried
      in the lapping path of water

without a worry where the river comes from
   or where it goes;
      something in me rises to meet

this ever-flowing fullness of the world—
   and what if every poem were a prayer,
      I muse, looking up

just in time to see a hawk,
   wide wings over the pines—
      there, just above the brow of the hill.

Notes

"Echo of the Former World"
This section title comes from the 2015 oil painting "Echo of the Former World" by George Carlson.

"Clementine"
The line "what I want to remember" refers to the question in the first line of William Stafford's poem "You Reading This, Be Ready," which asks, "Starting here, what do you want to remember?"

"Early on the River"
This section title comes from the title of a 2010 oil painting by John Evans.

"What Goes Among the Things That Change"
The title refers to a line in William Stafford's poem "The Way It Is."

"Haying Time"
The section title comes from the title of a 1928 oil painting by Oscar Berninghaus. This painting is one of many Berninghaus painted in the Taos Valley.

"Doing the Jigsaw Puzzle"
The jigsaw puzzle referred to in this poem lists the title of the painting on the puzzle box as "Van Gogh's

Sea at Sainte-Maries." The actual painting in the Van Gogh Museum, Amsterdam is titled *Seascape near Les Saintes-Maries-de-la-Mer.*

In the fourth stanza, "mackerel light" references a letter to his brother Theo in which van Gogh wrote that the Mediterranean "has a color like mackerel, in other words, changing—you don't always know if it's green or purple—you don't always know if it's blue—because a second later, its changing reflection has taken on a pink or grey hue." Vincent van Gogh to Theo van Gogh. 3–4 June 1888, The Letters. Van Gogh Museum, http://www.vangoghletters.org/vg/letters/let619/letter.html.

Acknowledgments

With gratitude to the editors and publishers of the following periodicals in which some of these poems appeared, sometimes in earlier versions:

Lips: "Elk," "Making Beds"

Patterson Review: "Letter Home"

Tiferet Journal: "Pockets of Stones" (as "For Virginia Woolf"), "What Goes Among the Things That Change"

"Letter Home" was awarded an Honorable Mention in the Allen Ginsberg Poetry Prize.

"All the Light in Between," "Anything with Wings," "Honey," "Instructions for Comfort Care," *"Let It Be Felt the Painter Was There"* (as "Homage to Pierre Bonnard"), "Letter Home," "Ode to a Boiled Egg," and "Quicksilver" were first published in the chapbook *All the Light in Between* (Finishing Line Press, 2013).

With Thanks

To Joan Cusack Handler, Gabriel Cleveland, Dimitri Reyes, Baron Wormser, Joy Arbor, and all at CavanKerry Press.

With appreciation for the sensibilities and insights of Laura Boss, Joan Brady, Raechel Bratnick, Elliot Figman, Maria Mazziotti Gillan, Suzanne Harris, Bambi Koeniger, Sinikka Laine, Leigh Rosoff, Donna Baier Stein, Frances Torrey, and especially to John, always my first reader. To my daughters, Alexandra, Kimberly, and Jennifer, for their grace and guidance, and to my son, Don, for his unfailing wit and wisdom.

Thanks to dear friends who bring me deeper into poetry each day.

To Poets & Writers, the Academy of American Poets, the Poetry Society of America, and *Tiferet Journal* for their dedication to inspiriting the wide community of writers.

With thanks to the New Jersey State Council on the Arts, the Geraldine R. Dodge Foundation, the Virginia Center for the Creative Arts, and the Vermont Studio Center.

CavanKerry's Mission

A not-for-profit literary press serving art and community, CavanKerry is committed to expanding the reach of poetry and other fine literature to a general readership by publishing works that explore the emotional and psychological landscapes of everyday life, and to bringing that art to the underserved where they live, work, and receive services.

Other Books in the Emerging Voices Series

Mausoleum of Flowers, Daniel B. Summerhill

A Half-Life, David S. Cho

Uncertain Acrobats, Rebecca Hart Olander

Her Kind, Cindy Veach

Deke Dangle Dive, Gibson Fay-LeBlanc

Pelted by Flowers, Kali Lightfoot

Rise Wildly, Tina Kelley

Set in Stone, Kevin Carey

Scraping Away, Fred Shaw

Rewilding, January Gill O'Neil

My Oceanography, Harriet Levin

See the Wolf, Sarah Sousa

Gloved Against Blood, Cindy Veach

Threshold, Joseph O. Legaspi

Jesus Was a Homeboy, Kevin Carey

Eating Moors and Christians, Sandra M. Castillo

Esther, Pam Bernard

Love's Labors, Brent Newsom

Places I Was Dreaming, Loren Graham

Misery Islands, January Gill O'Neil

Spooky Action at a Distance, Howard Levy

door of thin skins, Shira Dentz

Where the Dead Are, Wanda S. Praisner

Darkening the Grass, Michael Miller

The One Fifteen to Penn Station, Kevin Carey

My Painted Warriors, Peggy Penn

Neighborhood Register, Marcus Jackson

Night Sessions, David S. Cho

Underlife, January Gill O'Neil

The Second Night of the Spirit, Bhisham Bherwani

The Red Canoe: Love In Its Making, Joan Cusack Handler

WE AREN'T WHO WE ARE and this world isn't either, Christine
    Korfhage

Imago, Joseph O. Legaspi

Through a Gate of Trees, Susan Jackson

Against Which, Ross Gay

The Silence of Men, Richard Jeffrey Newman

The Disheveled Bed, Andrea Carter Brown

The Fork Without Hunger, Laurie Lamon

The Singers I Prefer, Christian Barter

Momentum, Catherine Doty

An Imperfect Lover, Georgianna Orsini

Soft Box, Celia Bland

Rattle, Eloise Bruce

Eye Level: Fifty Histories, Christopher Matthews

GlOrious, Joan Cusack Handler

The Palace of Ashes, Sherry Fairchok

Silk Elegy, Sondra Gash

So Close, Peggy Penn

Kazimierz Square, Karen Chase

A Day This Lit, Howard Levy

In the River of Songs has been set in Skolar Sans Latin typeface, a sans serif font selected to evoke a casual and relaxing tone throughout these poems. It was created by David Březina and Sláva Jevčinová for Rosetta Type Foundry.